MW01131185

opyright © 2017 by Sandeep Reddy

ll rights reserved. No part of this publication may be reproduced, distributed, or
ansmitted in any form or by any means, including photocopying, recording, or
ther electronic or mechanical methods, without the prior written permission of
ie author, except in the case of brief quotations embodied in critical reviews
nd certain other non-commercial uses permitted by copyright law. For
ermission requests, write to the author, at the e-mail address below.
mail: docsunny50@gmail.com

PREFACE

As thousands of students commence their PhD journeys each year, one thing is common to all these students: the uncertainty of completing their studies successfully. Unlike many other postgraduate programs, PhD students are largely on their own in navigating their studies. The students having to deal with significant academic and personal challenges can complicate circumstances. Of course, the home university and the supervisors may offer some level of support, but there is a general expectation that a PhD student work through his study program autonomously. This expectation and the candidate's context create a unique paradigm.

In an ideal situation, a full-time PhD student is expected to complete their program in three to four years* from start to finish (enrolment to examination results). However, completion of studies in this time frame can be difficult with many students taking much longer time to complete. The extended time frames can be due to several reasons ranging from inability to obtain research results in time to additional time required to wrap up their thesis writing. Sadly in some instances, PhD students drop out of the program midway. These situations shouldn't in most instances occur if proper planning is undertaken and the candidate is determined to complete their studies.

I aim, through this book, to guide PhD students to complete their studies in an effective and efficient manner. The motivation for writing this book comes from my own experience of completing PhD studies in a period of two years and three months' full-time equivalent** in challenging circumstances. This book provides information in a direct and easy-to-read manner while relying on scientific principles of learning. It is intended for the book to be read as whole but the structure of the book also lends itself to be read at different stages of the PhD journey. The content of this book has been presented in the context of the Australian and New Zealand PhD framework. However, the techniques discussed in this book should apply to any PhD program in the world.

Wishing you the best for your PhD studies,

Dr Sandeep Reddy MBBS DPH MSc MMgmt PhD

* In Australia and NZ.
** Four years and six months' part time.

CONTENTS

CHAPTER 1-PhD in a Nutshell

What is a PhD?

First, let us be on the same page as to what is a PhD program? PhD is the short term for a 'Doctor of Philosophy'. PhD can sometimes be abbreviated as DPhil. A PhD is the highest university qualification a student can achieve with some exceptions. In some countries like the UK and Germany, one can achieve a higher degree than PhD. These degrees are however uncommon and as it stands a PhD qualification is the terminal degree in most countries. Completion of a PhD means the student has demonstrated the necessary competencies to function as an independent researcher. This competency is proven by extensive and original contribution to the student's field of research during their studies.

Generally, it takes about three to four year's full time to complete a PhD, but the duration may differ depending on the student's individual circumstances and the country in which you are enrolled in the PhD program. For instance, the average duration for completion of PhD studies in Australia and New Zealand is three to four years while in the USA it is five to six years. This is because; in the USA there is a requirement to complete coursework before continuing into the research component. This requirement adds to the duration of PhD studies. This requirement does not apply in most instances in Australia and New Zealand PhD programs as it is expected that admitted students have acquired necessary skills to undertake research in the chosen field of study.

In the first year of a PhD the student, following discussions with the supervisory panel, prepares a research proposal- a plan outlining how the student intends to collect data/obtain results for and analyse the same with associated time frames. It is also generally expected that an extensive literature review be undertaken in this year and presented to your supervisors. In the second year the student embarks on collecting research data or laboratory results. You may during this year present some of your results in conferences or seminars. In the third year with all having gone smoothly in the previous years, you write up your research findings in the form of a thesis. However, in reality, these time frames are not necessarily adhered to. It is, therefore, the purpose of this book to enable you to follow these timelines as far as possible.

What are the different types of PhDs?

Figure I. A PhD can be studied in different ways.

As we discussed PhD programs differ by country but the format of studying and completing PhD can differ within a country by each University. The most common way of completing a PhD is starting afresh with a research project and collecting data to support your research statement followed by writing up of your thesis. We will discuss this PhD route throughout this book. However, it is pertinent to discuss here an alternative PhD route. Some universities offer a 'PhD by Publication' route for PhD applicants. Some universities require applicants to have substantial prior research and publication history but some other universities do not. So what is involved in this PhD study?

This type of PhD involves the candidate producing a series of publication ready articles or published articles, which take the place of traditional chapters in a thesis. The publications can be book chapters too. The publications are wedged between two substantial chapters-the introductory and conclusion chapters. While each article in the thesis can be read on their own there needs to be continuity or link across all the chapters/articles in the thesis. It is usually expected that you are the first author of all the publications and the articles written after your PhD enrolment. It is also expected the publications still meet the requirements for completing a PhD such as substantial, original contribution to the knowledge in discipline and meet conventional referencing standards.

There are several advantages in undertaking this type of PhD. An academic career, nowadays, is very much defined by publications. By publishing when you are undertaking your PhD itself gives you a head start. Publishing early provides you the skills to write and publish, thus helping your academic career later on. As publishing is a central feature in this PhD route you won't be able to push aside publishing for other considerations as you do with PhD by conventional routes. Also, completing your PhD through this pathway gives you the valuable experience of dealing with journals and the peer review process, which again will benefit your emerging academic career. Further considering each publication as a mini-project helps in completing your PhD pragmatically.

There are some disadvantages with this route. A main disadvantage is the time taken for journals to accept and publish your articles. There is a good possibility your submissions may be rejected by journals requiring major revision or alteration of your research. As there is no option but to publish in this pathway and with a general expectation to publish in quality journals there is bound to be immense pressure on the candidate. However, some universities allow journal ready publications to be included in the thesis i.e. articles before they are accepted in a journal. The other limitation is that some academics and universities perceive completion of your PhD through this route as less credible than the conventional PhD route.

Outline of a typical PhD program

With a PhD by thesis, the below program or route is usually followed.

- *Application and Enrolment*: In this phase, you chose a PhD program to enrol. This involves meeting the eligibility requirements of the University and program and finding an appropriate primary supervisor to guide you through the course.

- *Course Work*: In some countries like the US, a candidate has to complete some short courses before commencing research. Elsewhere the candidate may be required to undertake a mix of generic and specific research oriented training offered by the University.

- *Research Plan and Literature Review*: Typically, a candidate has to outline a plan for completing their PhD and the associated research process to the satisfaction of the supervisory panel. This is followed by extensive literature review about their chosen research topic.[1]

- *Data Collection*: Immaterial of where and what field the PhD is associated with this component applies universally. However, depending on the chosen topic the time involved in completing this phase may vary.

- *Thesis Writing*: One does not have to wait for the final stages of the PhD to commence writing the thesis. In fact, as we discuss later commencing writing early on helps. You could complete some preliminary chapters in the early phases of the PhD and progress them as your research evolves.

- *Dissemination of your Research*: This can take many forms. The most popular method is to present at conferences and seminars. Other students use media to promote important findings from their research. However, publication in peer-reviewed journals beats all of these methods. While it is difficult to publish in parallel to your studies as we discuss later this aspect is highly encouraged.

- *Submission and Examination*: Depending on the University, the submission and examination process will vary. However, generally in Australia and New Zealand following submission of your completed thesis, external examiners grade the thesis for its original contribution to the relevant research field and the quality of content. In other countries, the examination may adopt an oral approach where you defend your thesis/research in front of an examiner panel.

---

[1] For some Sciences, an extensive literature review may not be required with the emphasis being about the research design.

- *Graduation*: Now that the examiners have deemed your thesis/research as of a PhD grade all that is left for you is to graduate. Why is the graduation aspect important? Because you cannot use your PhD qualification or the 'Doctor' title until only after you officially graduate (in person or in absentia).

In the rest of this book we will spend more time on each of these phases especially on areas that you need to prioritise to complete your PhD faster or efficiently.

CHAPTER 2-Start with the Topic

Why is the research topic important?

The research topic of your PhD study (PhD topic) is a very important aspect of your PhD journey because of several reasons. The topic is something you will be researching for many years thus influencing your research plan (methodology and methods) heavily. The topic will also in many instances determine who will be your supervisor. Further, it being a PhD-level topic it establishes you as a subject expert in the area upon completion of your studies. Finally, the topic will be a key reference point in organising your time and resources throughout your PhD studies. Therefore, identifying a suitable and manageable topic becomes an important concern in the early stages of your PhD.

Think ahead

When choosing a research topic, two important considerations override others. These two considerations require you to think ahead and not just for the moment. One consideration is will the topic you have chosen sustain interest in the years you take to complete your PhD? After the initial excitement of commencing research on your topic in the first year, will the topic continue to trigger passion in the following years? Is the topic something you want to be associated with, in the form of the thesis and publications, into the future? Will you be satisfied the topic to define your term as an independent researcher? These are some of the questions one has to ask when identifying and confirming a topic for your PhD study.

The second consideration is to make the topic manageable for you to address and complete within the timeframes allocated for your PhD study. This means narrowing a broad research area to a research question that you feel confident to address. Many PhD students taken up by their excitement at the early stages bite off more they can chew by choosing a very broad or complex topic. This can prove unfortunate as students struggle to find answers to the research question or complete their research within the timeframes of their

PhD study. A majority of PhD students are not intending to gain a Nobel for their PhD research but rather want to complete their PhD or establish themselves as independent researchers or aid their academic career. On the flip side, you would also want to ensure the topic is not too narrow that it makes your study lightweight i.e. does not make a substantial contribution to the research field you have chosen. Because of these reasons, it is essential for you to review your research topic/question at the beginning of your PhD. Ask yourself if you can collect enough data to address the research question and write a meaningful thesis within the timeframes of your PhD study? Is the topic too broad or too complex to make it a practical topic? If so, can you review it with your supervisor/s to make it more manageable?

Research your research topic

Figure II. Investigate your topic.

After you have taken in the above considerations and before you finalise your research topic some more steps need to be taken. In some instances, University Departments recruit PhD candidates to research a specific topic. As funding is associated with the topic, there is little wiggle room for the candidate to change focus. However, most other times PhD candidates have an opportunity to pursue research in an area they are passionate about (as long it is within a field which aligns with their prior academic qualifications or professional experience). In this case, the candidate has to adopt certain precautions before committing to the research topic.

Some steps were discussed in the above section. In addition to this, the candidate has to check if a PhD hasn't been undertaken about the same topic. The candidate can use the University liaison librarian to help them with this aspect. Also, the supervisor panel who are usually experts in their fields will be able to advise you on the topic. Even if there has been a PhD study about the same topic, there is no cause for alarm. If the candidate still wants to pursue the same research topic, the candidate in discussion with their supervisor can modify the topic to such an extent that it does not come across as duplication of a completed study.

The other consideration while choosing a research topic is the resources required to complete the study. We discussed time frames earlier, but the other resource aspects are travel, accommodation and laboratory equipment if relevant. Will these costs be covered through PhD or University funds? If not, what are alternative funding sources? My experience has been that costs involved in field data collection can be substantial and taking this into account when developing your research topic is critical. The final piece in confirmation of the topic is the methodology required to research it. In some science related topics, the determination of methodology is straightforward, but in many cases, the topic determines the methodology and methods. So, you need to ensure you are comfortable with the methodology and methods involved to research your topic.

CHAPTER 3-University, University

Identifying the right university

Why is identifying a right university for your PhD studies important and should it be the only consideration? First, let me answer the latter part of the question. No, the university itself isn't the only consideration in choosing the location or platform for your PhD studies. Some PhD studies are not necessarily delivered through a conventional university framework; though some form of affiliation with a university is necessary to award the PhD degree. Also, there are many other factors than the university, which enable completion of your PhD. However, choosing the right university can arguably be the most important factor about the quality of your learning and the support you receive during your PhD studies. Also, the choice of the university has a significant bearing on your post-doctoral career whether it is academic or non-academic.

Figure III. Enrolling in the right university is important.

So how does one identify the right university for PhD study? There are a couple of tools you can use. One popular approach is to review the world ranking of the University. Currently, there are three widely accepted ranking frameworks. These are the Times Higher Education (THE) World University Rankings, QS World University Rankings and Academic Ranking of World Universities (ARWU). Results for universities are updated each year by these agencies and are published on their websites. The rankings are also generally categorised by region, discipline and age of the university. A potential PhD student can review their choice of the University for several variables including research outputs, student to staff ratio, student satisfaction, internationalisation...etc. Universities are increasingly giving importance to these rankings as they relay a particular image of their institution to potential students and employees.

However, these rankings have some limitations. There are far more universities in the world than these rankings cover or profile. Only a few performance indicators are used to calculate rankings, and these indicators vary across the ranking frameworks. So, a university ranked high in one ranking framework may not score well in another. While some of the ranking frameworks cover individual disciplines, they do not rank at the department level. A department is where you will be undertaking your PhD. While a university may have a good rank, it doesn't necessarily mean the department you are interested is good! Notwithstanding these limitations, approaching the rankings as the first point of call in identifying the right university is recommended.

An alternative route to home into the right university or department is to review the research activities occurring in your discipline. Where is this research occurring? Is it within a university department? Does the department allow and support PhD studies? What is the reputation of the department and university? These are some of the questions that need to be explored with this option. Through this route, you will have certainty that you will be pursuing a PhD in your preferred research area and in the right environment. However, there are some other factors you need to take into account with this option. We will discuss these in the following chapters.

Another option is to explore PhD scholarships. In many instances, PhD topics are predetermined for these scholarships as these scholarships are derived from research grants to the faculty. Generally, these scholarships not only cover university fees but also provide a monthly allowance for living costs. In some instances, these scholarships provide for airfare/relocation costs. A good website to identify such scholarships is https://www.findaphd.com The main limitation with this option is that you have little choice in developing your research topic if the topic is predetermined. Also, there are minimal options if you decide you want to change the focus of your PhD study. So, you are stuck with the predefined topic throughout your PhD studies. However, a potential student can apply for a general PhD scholarship through the University and not be bound to a particular topic.

One can also identify the right place to undertake PhD studies through networking. Approach post-doctoral candidates in your discipline and ask them about their PhD experiences. Did they find their study supported by the University/Department? Would they recommend you undertaking PhD studies in that particular University/Department? You can also approach the department directly and ask about support structures available for PhD students. If you can't approach an ex-PhD student or the department directly, you can seek advice or review experiences of current or ex-PhD students through online PhD forums such as these:

http://www.postgraduateforum.com/
https://www.findaphd.com/advice/phd-discussion-forum.aspx
https://www.phdstudent.com/recent.

A word of caution with these forums is to be careful about who you are getting advice from. Not all advice provided in these forums are credible, and one has to take each piece of advice cautiously.

The above options are not the only routes to choosing the right university/department but are the most practical approaches. My experience in choosing where I had to study has involved a mix of these options. However, my most important consideration was the profile of the department rather than the university. This meant reviewing the profiles of the academic staff in the department and investigating their availability to supervise. I also had conversations with ex-PhD students from the department to ensure I was able to pursue the research topic I had in mind through the department. Further to this, I reviewed the University enrolment process and support structures for higher degree research students, but this was investigated only after I was convinced about the department.

CHAPTER 4-Supervisor Rules

Choosing the right supervisor

It can't be emphasised enough how important a supervisor is in your PhD journey. While the University, Department and your personal circumstances play a very important role in progressing your PhD studies; they arguably take a back seat to the role of the primary supervisor. Your supervisor can make or break your PhD. Though studies at the level of PhD are supposed to be self-directed or autonomous studies, fortunately, or unfortunately your primary supervisor determines to a large extent how you progress and complete your PhD. This factor is mainly because of the University framework, which requires the involvement of the supervisor at crucial junctures like confirmation of candidature, annual reviews, appointment of supervisory and examiner panels, and approval of thesis for submission. Depending on your discipline, the supervisor also dictates the boundaries and direction of your research. While associate supervisors provide an alternate source of advice, key responsibilities with regards to your candidature rest with the primary supervisor alone. Therefore, finding an appropriate primary supervisor and managing the supervisor are critical elements in your PhD study!

So how do you find the right supervisor? There are a couple of tested routes. Just as you were encouraged to research your topic before committing to it, you are also encouraged to undertake some research about your potential supervisor. In some instances, a student may have completed a Masters by research or Bachelor Honours degree where they may have already been exposed to a supervisor, who is also "qualified"[2] to be a primary supervisor. If the academic is willing to supervise and the student is comfortable in continuing their PhD in the same university, they have it easy in choosing a "right" supervisor. Even then, due diligence must be undertaken before committing to the supervisor. You need to ensure the supervisor is the right

---

[2] Many universities require PhD primary supervisors to have completed a certain number of years of PhD supervision or supervised PhD students to their completion before they can qualify to be a primary supervisor.

academic to supervise your chosen research topics. Many times, a capable supervisor may not have the expertise to supervise your research topic. In other instances, a high-profile researcher whom you have had minimal interaction with during your Master's studies may not be a capable supervisor. Inquiries in these areas will help confirm your choice for a supervisor.

Those looking for supervisors in a different university have other options. Though, "research" is again the key word. If you have the luxury of developing your research topic i.e. not being encumbered by a predetermined research topic, you can search for leading researchers in your topic area. Review publications in your topic area and authors of these publications. Are these authors available as PhD supervisors? If yes, organise a meeting with the relevant academics and explicitly ask if they can support you throughout your PhD studies. One of the common and grievous mistakes PhD students make is not to be bold in stating their expectations. We will discuss this further in the next section, but it is important to have this conversation with a potential supervisor. It is only after the confirmation of support that you sign up with them as a supervisor. The risk in signing up with a non-committed supervisor can't be underestimated!

Regarding the experience of the supervisor, it is wise to have a seasoned supervisor. The supervisor not only has to guide you in your research but also negotiate the administrative process associated with your PhD including roping in suitable examiners at the time of your thesis. However, do not discount less experienced supervisors if they have the relevant expertise in your topic area. Many times, the advantage with these kinds of supervisors is they have more time to devote to your PhD, as they are likely to have a relatively lesser number of PhD students to supervise.

Sometimes, some PhD scholarships and projects, especially the laboratory based research projects, are tagged to a primary supervisor. This leaves you, if you are a scholarship holder, with minimal options in choosing your primary supervisor. In this case, ensure you have some associate supervisors to complement your primary supervisor.

Manage your supervisor!

Finding and confirming the right supervisor is half the story. As PhD is a long duration study, the ongoing relationship with your primary supervisor plays an important role in completing your studies. If you have taken the appropriate steps, as outlined in the previous section, to identify an appropriate supervisor; it is likely your relationship with the primary supervisor will have minimal hitches. However, what if there is a change with your supervisor? What if you haven't had a choice in choosing your supervisor? What if your "ideal" supervisor turns out to be "not so ideal" later on in your studies? This makes the relationship with your supervisor tricky and important to carefully manage.

Figure IV. Having a good relationship with your supervisor is essential.

The key to having a problem-free relationship with your supervisor is creating a structure of predictability. What does this mean? This means taking appropriate steps to ensure there is good and regular communication between yourself and your supervisor through an agreed meeting schedule. It is also important to ensure, within this framework, there is a proper understanding of each other's expectations. One way to organise this predictability is to develop a formal agreement at the commencement of your PhD studies. The agreement between yourself and your supervisor will outline the expectations, meeting schedules, alternate arrangements and support for your studies. While it may be difficult in some instances to bring up the notion of a formal agreement with your supervisor, it can't be stressed enough how vital such an arrangement (or it's equivalent) is to ensure you have a largely predictable relationship with your supervisor. Of course, there will be unexpected events such as change in supervisors or change with the research topic or interruption with your studies. A formal arrangement provides a sound platform to build an ongoing relationship with your supervisor.

While a formal arrangement sets you off on a good start, there are other initiatives you will need to take to manage the relationship with your supervisor. One aspect is to discuss which areas of your research will require your primary supervisor's involvement and which will require the associate supervisor's involvement. It is important to clarify this delineation as it may cause confusion and strife if you get conflicting research advice from your supervisors. Generally, the primary supervisor sets the direction of your research while allowing for you to consult the associate supervisor about sub-components of the research. It is very unusual for this to be reversed. In fact, if you are in such a situation, the recommendation is to change your supervisory arrangements as fast as possible.

Supervisors are humans too, which means they come with emotions and frailties. It is very rare for your supervisor relationship to be excellent throughout your PhD studies. It is critical you know how to anticipate and adapt to the personality of your supervisor. Some supervisors can be friendly to the point of being intrusive and others so distant that you feel you have a robot as a supervisor. Others may view you as a step to academic progression as universities increasingly expect student supervision from research academics. While other supervisors may want to use your PhD study as a testing platform for their theories. Therefore it is important to convey to your supervisor that you expect professional boundaries are maintained, academic competencies are acknowledged and suitable autonomy and support is provided at critical stages of your studies. Issues, if any, can be addressed through the earlier discussed formal arrangement mechanism but also through the university research student division.

In the worst-case scenario, if you have got to a point where the relationship with your supervisor is irreconcilable, the best course is to seek support from the university to change your supervisor/s. It will be foolish, unless in rare circumstances, to quit your PhD studies because of relationship issues with your supervisor.

Jake is in the second year of his PhD studies, at Trumble Town University, focusing on empirical modelling of commodity markets. His supervisor Professor Burton is a world-leading expert on empirical modelling using computational techniques. Jake was excited at the commencement of his PhD studies that Professor Burton had accepted to be his supervisor. However, Jake has lately been having several issues with his supervision. Professor Burton's expertise did not extend to financial and commodity markets, so Jake had to include an Associate Supervisor to guide him in this area. However, the Associate Supervisor now wants Jake to take a different approach in his study than what Professor Burton intends. With Professor Burton's frequent unavailability because of conference travel or modelling consultancies, Jake has been feeling isolated and worried about the direction of his PhD study.

Jake discusses the above issues with the Office of Graduate Research in his University and seeks a meeting with Professor Burton and his associate supervisor together. At the meeting Jake discusses the direction of his research and both the supervisors come to an agreement about an appropriate focus. At the same meeting, Jake discusses a schedule to have regular meetings between himself and his supervisors. He also seeks permission to participate in a couple of courses and seminars that will help with his studies. A meeting schedule and Jake's participation in relevant courses is agreed to by Professor Burton. Jake is now feeling confident and optimistic about his prospects of completing his PhD study.

CHAPTER 5-The Plans that Rule them All

Drafting a Plan

Undertaking a PhD study is not a trivial task and depending on the context can be the most complex and time-consuming task you will be involved with. Such an activity will need appropriate planning to factor in generic and specialised tasks to progress your studies. There are two plans you will need to develop. One plan is generic covering the administration, support activities and milestones associated with your PhD. The other one relates how you approach your research (methodology, methods and analysis). Some combine both plans but is easier to follow the plans if the activities are separated.

General Plan

This plan covers milestones and deadlines that are prescribed by the University. I will call it the 'General Plan', but you can call it the 'PhD Milestone Plan' or the 'Activity Plan' or whatever suits you. However, a distinction must be drawn between this plan and the 'Research Plan', which is a plan on how you collect and analyse your research data and doesn't cover other data such as PhD course and administration related data. To develop the general plan, you would need to, as an overview, outline the number of years you have scheduled for your PhD studies. For example, a full-time PhD will have three or four years and if part-time, it will be six or eight years. Within each year and by month, you outline important activities and relevant milestones that have to be completed that year. It could be developing a research proposal[3] and a thesis outline. Also, scheduled reviews such as annual review are to be factored in. Further, the plan can cover planned meetings or events in the university such as scholarship, seminars and course advisory meetings. Also planned meetings with your supervisor/s can be written in.

Consider, important family commitments and holidays in the plan as they can

---

[3] Sub-activities such as literature review and methodology are to be covered in the research plan not here.

impact on the progress of your studies. Each activity and milestone can then be colour coded to indicate the level of importance. An example plan is illustrated below:

Year 1	Jan	Feb	Mar	Apr	May	Jun	Jul	Aug	Sep	Oct	Nov	Dec
University related activity	University Orientation										Annual Review	
Supervisor related activity	Preliminary Supervisor Panel Meeting											
PhD study related activity		Commence Research Proposal							Complete Research Proposal	Obtain Approval for Proposal	Commence Thesis Outline	
Personal activity						Holiday	Holiday					

Figure V. Example of a Year 1 General Plan.

The figure is an example for Year 1. Similar plans can be developed for each year of your PhD study.

Research Plan

This plan is to inform how you undertake your PhD research including the scope of research work, research tasks and time frames. It is not an outline for your research proposal or thesis (we will discuss the thesis in a later chapter) but a framework for how you conduct your research. The plan is outlined below:

Year 1

Research Activity	Jan	Feb	Mar	Apr	May	Jun	Jul	Aug	Sep	Oct	Nov	Dec
Literature Review	Commence				Complete							
Research Proposal						Commence						Complete

Year 2

Research Activity	Jan	Feb	Mar	Apr	May	Jun	Jul	Aug	Sep	Oct	Nov	Dec
Recruitment	Commence			Complete								
Data Collection					Commence							Complete

Year 3

Research Activity	Jan	Feb	Mar	Apr	May	Jun	Jul	Aug	Sep	Oct	Nov	Dec
Data Analysis	Commence					Complete						
Thesis Writing									Commence			

Year 4

Research Activity	Jan	Feb	Mar	Apr	May	Jun	Jul	Aug	Sep	Oct	Nov	Dec
Thesis Writing					Complete							

Figure VI. Example of a PhD Research Plan.

Together the general and research plan form a good framework to schedule and implement your PhD related research and administrative activities. The plans also help you to track your progress towards completion and act as reminders if you are falling behind. However, be open to change elements and timeframes within the plans if you are faced with unplanned eventualities.

CHAPTER 6-Organising Your Life

Life Happens

We all want to be in control of our life. So do PhD students who not only want to be in control of their studies but also the events that affect their studies. However, in reality, many circumstances are beyond our control. If the PhD student is not prepared to manage or how they react to these events, they can severely impact the progression of their studies. Sometimes even leading to students forgoing their studies. This shouldn't be. Universities and most supervisors are now becoming more understanding of student's circumstances. Support is being offered by universities through various channels to sustain the motivation and progression of students. However, at the end of the day, it is your PhD and you will need to take charge of the plan and progression of your studies. This means you need to know how to organise your studies and life to support the completion of your study.

Full-Time Student

On the surface, a full-time PhD student has it all going i.e. All of your working hours dedicated to studying, perhaps a scholarship added in to take care of the pesky financial issues, and if located on the campus direct access to your supervisors. These factors should keep you progressing in your studies; right? Yes and No! Yes, these factors give a full-time student a distinct advantage over a part-time PhD student balancing work commitments with PhD commitments. No, because a full-time PhD student is nowadays likely to have other commitments beyond his PhD studies. It is likely the scholarship, even if a full one, is not enough to cover the entire student's expenses, so the student has taken up part-time work within or outside the university. If you are a fee-paying full time student, you may require to work to cover your expenses. Perhaps, the student has a family especially common amongst international students and those who take up their PhD studies late. Maybe, an unexpected event leads to the student switching from a full-time mode to a part-time mode? All these issues can definitely have an impact on a full-time student's motivation and progression.

Part Time Student

Part-time PhD studies are increasingly becoming common with many students undertaking studies alongside full time work. Coupled with work commitments, the part-time student usually has family commitments too. The part time PhD student, to be frank, has a clear disadvantage compared to a full time PhD student. The disadvantage is compounded if you are undertaking your studies from a different location as that of your university and supervisor. While part time students get a longer period to complete their studies, the lengthy period can also lead to complacency and less motivation than a full time student. As they are working full time, time allocation for PhD studies may be inadequate leading to less than an ideal progression of their studies. Further to this, family commitments can draw away from whatever little time they have allocated to their studies. It is said the longer the time taken by a part time PhD student, the less likely they are to complete their study!

The Answers

There is no grand solution or a magic wand you can whip up to make the aforementioned issues vanish. However, non-study commitments can be managed, and unexpected events appropriately responded to. I completed my PhD studies as a part-time student while working full-time with no study leave. Coupled with this I had significant family and professional commitments leaving very little time for my PhD study. It is the way you adapt to your circumstances and make the best of them that marks you out for success. Reviewing successful PhD completions, I have identified persistence, planning and pragmatism as the three key themes that defined their success.

When you juggle multiple commitments, it is important to delineate the other commitment from your PhD studies. Reserve aside a dedicated day/time for your study. As far as possible, do let not other obligations intrude into this space. Be strict about sharing this important time with other encroaching issues if you are keen on completing your studies on time. Create a monthly timetable, using ideas derived from the previous chapter, identifying the work, life, and study objectives you have for the month. Then ensure you allocate time, which you pragmatically see as less likely to be intruded into, for your PhD study. If at all some unexpected event keeps you away from your studies; confirm you can catch-up with things you are behind with by allocating extra time for your studies in your monthly schedule. Importantly, guarantee you continue with this scheduling/allocation throughout your studies.

If you are undertaking studies alongside full-time work, ensure you speak to your employer about your study commitment. Some organisations, especially educational institutions, allow for their employees to take regular study leave and even pay the necessary study fees. If a formal study leave can't be obtained, negotiate a schedule that allows you to reserve time for your PhD studies. For those with families, a similar approach in negotiating a regular period with your family members for your study becomes vital. I wasn't able to obtain study leave, during my PhD studies, but reserved part of my weekend for PhD studies and negotiated with my family members to allow me that period to progress my studies undisturbed.

Figure VII. Balancing your study with other commitments is essential.

A key reason for part time students losing interest/motivation with their studies is the perception of 'isolation'. Many part time students are undertaking their PhD studies from a different location with limited access to physical resources and their supervisors. Many support services or seminars that are held on campus may not be available for distance students. One can see how this 'distance' can affect studies. However, in the current times, geographical distance has been overcome by virtual proximity. Library resources can be accessed digitally. The seminar can be made accessible post event for students through recordings. Meetings with supervisors can be organised via video or telephonic modes. Virtual groups, comprising part time or distance PhD students, can be formed or membership sought. These measures coupled with timed visits to the campus can diminish the sense of isolation for distance or part-time PhD students. Also a part-time student has to be proactive in scheduling regular meetings with their supervisors to ensure their studies are on track and align with the supervisor's expectations. The meetings are especially important at the beginning and towards the end of the student's studies.

Full-time students can also be affected by isolation if they are away from their families or in a different country or not well connected to their supervisors or disconnected to their research topic. Chapter 2 discussed how to develop and maintain interest in a study topic. Chapter 4 discussed the relationship with your supervisor. In addition to these discussed solutions, it is important to benefit from university support services as much as possible. Nearly all universities have professional counselling services that students can access on campus or remotely. It is important to avail these services if you feel the need to open up in a confidential and safe environment. The significance of these sessions in decreasing the isolation and perking up the student, especially at times when they are feeling demotivated or stressed, can't be emphasised enough. Also, on campus students can join cultural or hobby student groups they identify with so they have some time where they can remove themselves from the pressure of studies and deadlines. Further, students can participate in campus based PhD support groups or research activities such as 3-minute thesis competitions and poster competitions to connect to fellow PhD students and showcase their research.

A PhD study, considering it's lengthy duration, doesn't have to be dull and depressing. Also, your studies shouldn't be keeping you away from important life events like births, marriages and funerals. As mentioned earlier, pragmatism, planning and persistence will ensure you respond to and manage expected and unexpected events appropriately.

Alice was a full-time PhD student at the University of Mackleshire researching transformability of low-lying islands in the Pacific Ocean in response to climate change. She had a good supervisory panel and an excellent relationship with her primary supervisor. She was currently in the third year of her PhD study, just having completed her field data collection from Solomon Islands. Unfortunately, with the sudden demise of her father and the ensuing poor health of her mother, she was required to move back to her hometown to provide care for her mother. This meant part-time distance PhD study. Alice was proactive in discussing with her primary supervisor where she stood in her completion of her PhD studies and fixing regular meetings with him, through remote video, to progress her remaining studies. She also accessed counselling services offered by the university to ensure she kept the big picture and the end goal in sight. With the support of her supervisors and the university, Alice was able to complete her PhD study as scheduled.

CHAPTER 7-Ethics Review: A Research Booster

Ethics Review

If your PhD research involves humans or data about them, in all likelihood your research will require ethics approval. The ethics application process is to be seen as an advantage to your study rather than a limiting step. The ethics review route will either help with strengthening or confirming your research strategy. The process provides an avenue for you to ensure your research is safe for participants, it has an appropriate research design, and you have a meaningful strategy to disseminate your research findings. In most instances, a nationally recognised human research ethics committee will receive your application for review and approval. Depending on your research, you will require both a university ethics committee and an organisational ethics committee to review your application. However, ethics committees are now adopting mutual recognition strategies to streamline and fasten the ethics approval process. What this means is once you receive ethics approval from a recognised external ethics committee, you will gain automatic approval from the university ethics committee. However, you will still need to formally approach the university ethics committee and provide evidence of approval from the external ethics committee before gaining its approval.

Ethics Application Process

So what is involved with the ethics application procedure? First, you need to determine if your research involves negligible risk or low risk or high risk. The risk is determined based on the inconvenience and harm to research participants. You can consult with your supervisor and the ethics committee secretariat to determine which of the risk categories your research is associated with. Based on the risk category, different application procedures are involved. If your research is negligible risk i.e. perceivably no harm to participants and only minor inconvenience is involved, your application may not have to go to the full committee and can be reviewed either by the chair or a sub-committee. However, if your research is deemed either as low or high risk, your application will require going through the full committee. Most human research ethics committees have dedicated webpages, where forms and guidelines for the application process are made available. After you have submitted your ethics application, the committee in it's meeting will review and make a decision about your application. Most applications, if well prepared, will receive conditional approval i.e. full approval when relevant amendments are made. While others will receive full approval and some others will be recommended for resubmission.

Figure VIII. Ethics review will strengthen your study.

Tips for obtaining ethics approval

There are some time-tested tips one can adopt to ensure ethics approval in a minimal time frame. These measures included good preparation, which involves planning for the ethics application process early into your PhD study, reviewing relevant application forms and guides, so you enter the right information and having your application reviewed by your supervisor and if possible another academic who has experience in submitting ethics applications. In addition to these steps, you will need to ensure you communicate clearly in your application. This means using plain language, as ethics committee members may not be experts in your area of research and some members may be lay members who do not have research expertise. When explaining your research place yourself in the committee member's or research participant's shoes. Will they understand what you are trying to convey? What issues they may see as precluding approval have to be adequately explained. Finally ensure you follow all the instructions specified on the committee's website, which includes ensuring the correct forms are used, and the application package is complete.

By completing the ethics application early into your PhD study, you will gain several benefits including a robust external peer review of your research proposal, safeguard for your research participants and confidence that you are undertaking good research. Some use the ethics committee approval as a basis to publish their protocol, which is another advantage of gaining ethics approval early on.

CHAPTER 8-The Handyman Tools

PhD tools

PhD study can be stressful, so support tools such as software programs that help with your research and thesis writing are welcome. Fortunately, numerous software, which helps a student's progress with their studies exist. However, one has to be shrewd in picking the right software if not the student will be wasting precious time and money. In this chapter, I have compiled a list of software programs, which I have found immensely useful in completing my PhD study. These software not only help with the organisation of your studies and data collection but also accelerate the pace of your studies considerably. I have covered only generic software in this list and not covered discipline-specific software, which can be important depending on the research you are conducting. For such software, either your supervisor or your department should be able to provide advice.

Reference Management

Immaterial of the discipline you are undertaking your PhD, you will need to cite your non-original content whether it be in your research proposal or literature review or Thesis. Gone are the days when you had to manually prepare a list of references and then cite them within the text using any of the established referencing conventions. Nowadays, several software programs that manage references and even host the relevant articles exist. Some are free, and some are available through subscription. Here I discuss two-reference management software that I found useful.

EndNote:

EndNote™

By far, EndNote is the most popular reference manager and is now offered through Clarivate Analytics (previously Thomson Reuters). For most PhD students the software is offered through the University system. This is good as the software is not available for free and costs a hefty sum if purchased independently. EndNote helps with organising your reference list, including importing and exporting of references. References are entered manually and you can specify the referencing convention they need to be set in. References can be organised in folders and the software also offers repository search. It also offers a preview of your selected reference so that one can check details of the reference.

Figure IX. EndNote User Interface.

EndNote is available for installation on your desktop but is also available on the cloud, which can synchronise with your desktop collection. This synchronisation means you can still access your reference list when you travel or when you don't have access to your personal computer. The other important feature of EndNote is you can cite references while you write by adding a plugin to Microsoft Word. Generally Universities offer EndNote training as part of their PhD student orientation, and it is highly recommended you participate in such training especially if you haven't been exposed to EndNote before.

Mendeley:

I started off with EndNote as most PhD students do as it was offered for free through the university system and because I had used EndNote before.

However, I started to find EndNote a bit clunky and not meeting my needs, so I started to explore other electronic reference managers. This was when I came across Mendeley reference manager.

As the basic version of Mendeley is offered free and came highly recommended by academics from Cambridge and John Hopkins universities; I went ahead and installed the software on my computer. As I could export my EndNote reference list to BibTex and then import the BibTex data to Mendeley, I did not have to create my reference list in Mendeley from scratch. Mendeley provides most of the features that you can avail from EndNote including folder organisation, repository search, ability to record references in different conventions, cite while you write and cloud synchronisation.

Figure X. Mendeley User Interface.

However, the main Mendeley features that stood out for me aside from it being available for free and it's agility and user-friendly interface are the ability to drag and drop a PDF version of an article and for Mendeley to extract the relevant elements to create a reference. Yes, the software does this. It doesn't get it right all the time but most of the times, the software does the work for you. It even checks with you if the reference construction is right. When you feel the construction is not right, you can manually edit the reference to make it right. As PDF documents can be saved in the Mendeley database, the software can also act as your PhD literature repository. I also found its ability to align with Microsoft Word as a plugin great to cite while I wrote my thesis. There are some drawbacks with the software like some large documents wouldn't open or would cause the software to crash, and importing and exporting features have yet to evolve at the level of EndNote. Universities do not generally offer support or training for Mendeley as EndNote monopolises the university system. However, for free software Mendeley is exceptional. I was able to have all my reference management needs for the most of the course of my PhD study addressed by Mendeley without a need to seek support from EndNote.

Literature Search

Like most university students you will be familiar with academic databases like PubMed, Web of Science, Scopus...etc. You will even have undergone training to search for literature in these databases. However, use of these databases can get confusing sometimes. Also, if you are not using the university network, access to these databases may not be possible. This is where free to access simplistic search tools come into play. Of these Google Scholar is something I found most useful.

Figure XI. Google Scholar User Interface.

Google Scholar has vastly improved since it was offered to the public and now searches across a broad range of scholarly literature including peer-reviewed articles, conference proceedings, texts and theses. It uses sources such as university websites, online repositories, professional organisations, and academic publishers. Google Scholar can also be accessed through the university system, and it is said this site yields better results. While PubMed and other academic databases are human-curated databases, Google Scholar is a search engine. The student has to understand this distinction as it has an impact on search results. Full-text articles may not be accessible through Google Scholar. Also, while Google Search offers the ability to customise search, academic databases offer a better capability to undertake advanced search. In my experience, I used Google Scholar as the first stop for literature search. After getting a feel of the literature that is available, I progressed to academic databases like PubMed and Web of Science if I needed to download full-text articles.

File Hosting

As your PhD study progresses and your need to save and share large document increases, you will realise that you can't be dependent on the university system to cater to this need. Flash discs and portable storage systems can address the mobility issue but have associated risks. File hosting on the cloud is increasingly becoming popular. Of this Dropbox is the most popular service.

Once you create an account (basic account is free), you can upload your documents to the Dropbox server and access the document wherever there is the Internet. The basic account has a limit on storage, but you can upgrade to gain more storage. Dropbox can also be installed on your personal computer or tablet and allow you to drop files into the Dropbox folder. I found Dropbox especially useful to share files of large capacity like my thesis amongst my supervisors who were based in different locations. I also used Dropbox as a backup server to ensure my research data was not lost if my laptop or computer crashed. If you are running out of space with a basic Dropbox account or you did not like Dropbox; alternate file hosting sites include OneDrive (for Windows users), Google Drive, Amazon Cloud Drive and

Box.com.

Editing

For some of you, English may be your second language and for some others writing in academic English may not comfortably sit with you. You are looking for some support with your writing especially grammar and syntax. Affording external editors may be expensive especially in the early years of your PhD study where there is no thesis allowance. Microsoft Word spell check has intrinsic weakness, and for a PhD, you require more than what spell check can offer. This is where 'Grammarly' helps.

The developers term Grammarly as a writing enhancement software and it is. I found Grammarly extremely useful in my studies as it provides multiple functions including grammar and syntax check and plagiarism detector. Because of the additional features like real-time suggestions to make your writing better and ability to integrate with Microsoft Office and web browsers, it is much more than Turnitin (a plagiarism detection software frequently used by universities). The basic version of Grammarly can be accessed for free, but the premium version, which checks for sentence structure, plagiarism, and integrates with Microsoft Word requires annual payments. While Grammarly is not perfect, my experience has been that it significantly enhances the quality of your writing.

Figure XII. Grammarly Web Interface.

Organisation

Finally, as we discussed in Chapters 5 and 6, PhD study requires careful planning and organisation. While there is always unpredictable stuff, appropriate task management does wonders for your PhD study progression. Wunderlist is a popular cloud-based task management application, which allows users to manage their tasks from different devices. Wunderlist was a big part of my PhD studies keeping me well organised and on track with my PhD milestones.

Wunderlist

Wunderlist, now owned by Microsoft, allows users to create task lists with associated deadlines. Wunderlist even suggests categories like 'Work' and 'Private' for you to add tasks to. Wunderlist allows collaboration amongst different users so you can share tasks and deadlines. Wunderlist also works across different operating systems with an ability to synchronise data to a cloud server. Wunderlist is available both as free and paid versions. However, the free version should satisfy most users.

CHAPTER 9- Data busting

Data Management

Data collection and analysis is a huge component in your PhD studies. Not only is an appropriate strategy to manage data important but so too is the right data collection and analysis tools about your study's methodology. The methodology you employ in your research (Quantitative or Qualitative or Mixed Methods) will determine the type of data and collection method. It is important to approach data collection and analysis methodically. Also, it is important to present the data suitably. We will briefly in this chapter discuss the different steps and methods involved in collection and analysis of data.

Figure XIII. Getting your data strategy right is critical.

Types of Data

First, I would like to bring to your attention the way of classifying research data i.e. primary and secondary data. This is separate to the categorisation of data as quantitative and qualitative data.

Primary data is the data that has been collected by you first-hand during your research. The data hasn't been collected for the same purpose before and published. As you have direct control over the data, you can usually be assured of the integrity and validity of the data. Secondary data, on the other hand, is data you have obtained from another published source or database. While there may be issues with the validity of the data sometimes, it can be an important source especially when you can't obtain the same data first hand.

Quantitative Data

Quantitative methodology mainly involves quantifying relationships between variables. The two main types of quantitative research are descriptive and experimental studies. With descriptive studies, the association between variables is established. While experimental studies involve establishing causation between variables. Descriptive studies usually comprise one-time measurement of a sample and experimental study design usually encompasses before and after testing of the hypothesis.

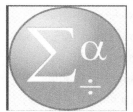 It is obvious from this description that quantitative research involves the collection of numerical data followed by statistical analysis. There are some important considerations in quantitative data collection including a need to classify and categorise data i.e. date and place of collection, type and unit of measurement and details of the sample from which data is collected. Usually, quantitative data collection requires a large sample (a large number of participants). Also, the emphasis on the analysis, especially if it is an experimental design is on the generalisability of findings. Findings can be presented in tabular format, like charts, like figures and other non-textual forms. For PhD students a popular software package that is frequently used for quantitative analysis is SPSS.

SPSS is a software program, owned and marketed by IBM that can be used for most varieties of quantitative analysis including descriptive statistics, bivariate statistics, the prediction for numerical outcomes and group identification. The software interface, similar to a Microsoft Excel spread sheet, is easy to use for beginners. Once data is entered into the software in the appropriate format, the program not only can undertake statistical analysis but also predictive modelling and data mining. While the interface is user-friendly, I still recommend using either your university resources or external avenues to obtain SPSS basic training. This is to ensure data is entered in the appropriate manner and you are choosing the appropriate statistical method to undertake the analysis.

Qualitative Data

Unlike quantitative methodology, in Qualitative research, the objective is to obtain an understanding of the experiences of participants. This means the researcher seeks to access the thoughts and feelings of participants and record the same in textual data. The size of the sample and generalisability of

findings is not critical here. However, as with quantitative research, structure and categorisation of data is critical. There are various ways of collecting qualitative data, but most qualitative research involves

interviews in one form or another. Interview data is recorded and transcribed to undertake the in-depth analysis. Analysis can be approached through different mechanisms but generally involves coding of data. Here coding means the classification of transcribed /textual data into a form understandable by computer software. The most often used software package in qualitative research for coding and analysis, especially thematic analysis is QSR NVivo.

NVivo is computer-aided qualitative data analysis software developed and marketed by QSR International. NVivo helps with organising qualitative data including textual and multi-media information and then analysing the same for relationships and themes. NVivo has other functions such as the ability to query and search data, create models, maps and graphs from the data and ability to share data and collaborate with fellow researchers. Unlike NVivo the interface takes some time to get used to, and at the minimum, a beginner requires some training to know how to use the software. Both universities and QSR provide basic and advanced training modules.

CHAPTER 10-Go Right about Writing

Writing for success

The importance of writing regularly during your PhD study can't be emphasised enough. Not only writing regularly but also very early into your PhD study is recommended. But what do you write; the thesis isn't due until the end of the PhD study? This is a frequent misconception on the part of most PhD students i.e. you do not have to commence writing until the final phases of your PhD studies. There are various components that require writing in the early stages of the PhD like your research proposal (covered in Chapter 2), research plan (covered in Chapter 5) and ethics application (covered in Chapter 7). The earlier you get into the habit of writing the better the chances are for your success i.e. completing your PhD.

However, it is not easy to write especially if you are not used to writing regularly or have other commitments. To an extent, the PhD student has to force himself/herself to write regularly. Reserving some time each week to write content related to your PhD research helps in developing this habit. The writing could be done through your research proposal framework or the thesis framework (see next section). Also, you could write notes about your supervisor meeting, participant recruitment, field visits and observations about the epistemology and methodology of your study. So there is no dearth of content to write even in the early stages of your PhD study.

Thesis

Another misconception the PhD students have is they do not have to commence work on their thesis until the final stages of their study. Sometimes supervisors promote this misconception by discouraging eager PhD students from beginning work on their thesis. However, as most people who have completed their PhD within recommended time frames will attest early attention to the thesis is important. You may ask what can I write in the thesis if I haven't commenced my data collection and analysis? There is plenty. As the figure XIV outlines, the student can commence writing the 'Introduction', 'Literature Review' and 'Methodology' chapters. The content can be derived from your finalised research proposal. I found it very helpful to prepare a draft version of my thesis as soon as I had my research proposal finalised. The early commencement of writing my thesis meant not only I had enough content to cover all the chapters but also I had enough time in the end to refine my thesis in the final stages of my PhD studies.

The outline provided below gives you a good framework to build your thesis. The outline may not suit certain study disciplines but will be relevant to most PhD studies. Good luck with your writing.

> ➢ **Title:** Concise, full name of author, current academic credentials, University, submitted to fulfil PhD, month, year.
>
> ➢ **Abstract:** Brief statement about problem/hypothesis, methodology, methods and findings.
>
> ➢ **Author's Declaration:** Declaration that the thesis is your original work.
>
> ➢ **Table of Contents**
>
> ➢ **List of Figures**
>
> ➢ **List of Tables**
>
> ➢ **Acknowledgements**
>
> ➢ **Introduction/Background:** Here you provide the context for your research, and a brief outline of what you will cover in the thesis.
>
> ➢ **Literature Review:** Here you provide a review of the literature/previous research pertaining to your study topic.
>
> ➢ **Position of Researcher:** Here you provide a brief summary of why you are undertaking this research i.e. justification for the research and if applicable your views of the ontology and epistemology behind the study.
>
> ➢ **Methodology:** Here you discuss the methodology (qualitative or quantitative or mixed) and methods employed to collect data and undertake analysis.
>
> ➢ **Findings/Results:** Here you present the findings/results of your research including tables and graphs.
>
> ➢ **Discussion:** Here you discuss the findings in relation to other studies and published literature and the implications of your findings for your discipline.
>
> ➢ **Conclusion:** Here your provide a summary of your thesis and suggest the way forward i.e. how can one build on your research.
>
> ➢ **Appendices**

Figure XIV. Suggested Thesis Outline.

CHAPTER 11-The End Game

Congrats, you are nearly there!

If you have arrived at the final stages of your PhD (i.e. thesis completion and examination stage), pat yourself on the back. You have done very well to come to this stage. You have had your research proposal confirmed, undertaken a major literature review, collected study data and analysed the same, brought on board your supervisors and navigated the work-life issues successfully. All of these no easy tasks by any measure. However, the final stages can also be the most stressful and uncertain stage of your PhD study experience. Fortunately, there are some time-tested methods and frameworks that you can adopt that will help you navigate this phase too.

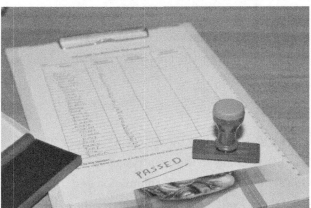

Figure XV. Adopting the right steps will lead to success.

Thesis

In the last chapter, we discussed a template/outline for drafting your thesis. Here we will discuss how to position the content of your thesis to maximise the chances of gaining positive reviews from your examiners.

The most important considerations any examiner will be looking for are the originality of your research and the contribution it is making to your discipline. If you don't get these two components right, it doesn't matter how nicely your thesis is formatted and how many hours you have spent on it. You won't gain traction from the examiners if you don't fulfil these criteria.

Emphasise these components in your thesis (recollect the 'position of researcher' chapter I suggested in the thesis outline where this could be emphasised. Also, the discussion chapter can provide a platform for this information). In addition to these two fundamental components, a sound and thorough literature review is required. The literature review should not only demonstrate that you have an appreciation of research and data relating to your research topic but also cover current and important references. A couple of other significant tips include you ensuring the methodology and methods you have chosen are appropriate to the research question you are pursuing and that your prose and formatting in the thesis is impeccable. There is no point in using methods and data that do not align with your research question and in fact, will lessen the credibility of your research. To ensure the appropriate formatting and grammar for your thesis, you can employ an external editor if your university permits and you have the budget for it. Nowadays, many PhD students even those who are Native English speakers employ editors to help with their thesis.

Exam

Finishing a well-drafted thesis does not mark the conclusion of your PhD study; there is yet the Exam! Depending on the country and university, the PhD can either be a written submission or an oral submission or a combination of both. In this book, I will focus on the written submission route common to Australia and New Zealand. The pre-examination period can be stressful, but it is important to ensure that you follow the university prescribed steps for examination. Usually, these steps involve gaining all of your supervisor's approvals to submit the thesis for examination, your supervisor identifying external examiners as per university rules, and you printing the final version of your thesis for examination. External examiners will generally remain anonymous to you but will be academics that have expertise in the relevant discipline.

Once you have submitted your thesis, via the University, for the examination you will have some waiting period for the examiners to return their reports. Examiners will be reviewing the thesis as per University recommended criteria, which usually aligns with the points mentioned in the previous section. There are different levels of grading's depending on the University, but usually , the grades are as follows:

- Passed- No requirement for corrections or amendments other than minor editorial changes.
- Passed- Subject to specific, minor amendments that are more than minor editorial changes.
- Revise and resubmit
- Failed

The good news is most PhD students if they have had approval from their supervisors to submit for examination will get either of the first two grades. It is very rare that PhD students receive either of the last two grades. If you have followed the steps outlined in the various chapters of this book, you should easily be gaining either of the first two grades. In the worst-case scenario, don't panic. You have come so far, so you shouldn't be giving up. You can still work with your supervisors and university to undertake a revision of the thesis based on examiner's feedback and resubmit either to the same examiner panel or a new one.

I hope the information outlined in this book will provide you with a clear and robust strategy not only to undertake your studies but also complete your PhD successfully. Best of Luck!

Brett is excited that he has completed the first draft of his thesis. He has spent three months drafting the thesis. He sends off the draft to his supervisor for feedback. The supervisor comments the thesis requires a significant revision. Alarmed, Brett meets with his supervisor to get more details. The supervisor advises while the presentation of the methodology, methods and findings were fine, the thesis had inadequate literature review and numerous formatting and grammatical errors. Brett takes on board the feedback and provides more content for his literature review. He also hires an external editor to help him with the formatting, grammar and syntax. Following these changes, he resubmits the thesis to his supervisory panel. They are all happy with the revised thesis and permit submission of the thesis for examination.

Index

Made in United States
North Haven, CT
31 August 2024

56812617R00029